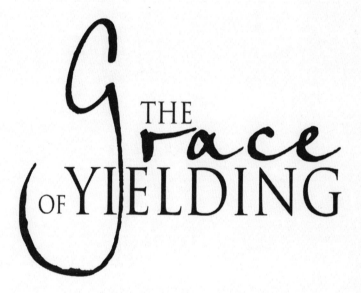

THE Grace OF YIELDING

Other Titles by Derek Prince

THE Grace OF YIELDING

DEREK PRINCE

W
WHITAKER
HOUSE

All Scripture quotations are taken from the King James Version of the Holy Bible.

THE GRACE OF YIELDING

Derek Prince
Derek Prince Ministries—International
P. O. Box 19501
Charlotte, NC 28219
www.dpmusa.org

ISBN: 0-88368-693-7
Printed in the United States of America
© 1977 by Derek Prince Ministries—International

Whitaker House
30 Hunt Valley Circle
New Kensington, PA 15068
www.whitakerhouse.com

Library of Congress Cataloging-in-Publication Data

Prince, Derek.
The grace of yielding / Derek Prince.
        p.   cm.
ISBN 0-88368-693-7 (pbk.)
1. Christian life.   I. Title.
BV4501.3 .P75 2001
248.4—dc21
2001003801

---

2 3 4 5 6 7 8 9 10 11 12   **W**   11 10 09 08 07 06 05 04

Contents

Introduction

The Lord has led me to write this book on the theme, *the grace of yielding.* Let me say, first of all, that there are some things to which, as Christians, we should never yield. I do not believe that we should ever yield to Satan, for the Scripture says, *"Resist the devil, and he will flee from you"* (James 4:7). Nor do I believe that we should ever yield to sin, for the sixth chapter of Romans tells us that we are not to yield our members to sin (verse 13). However, there are circumstances and situations that occur in our lives that are only resolved when we learn to yield.

I have found that knowing how to yield is a mark of maturity that I look for in myself and that I esteem in others. I was listening just recently to a young preacher whom God has greatly blessed. He is a fine young man, and God has done a great deal for him. But the whole theme of this man's preaching was what *he* could do, not what God could do. All of it was true, and all of it was good. But I was sitting there saying to myself, "Brother, I'll be interested to see you come to the end of that."

There is a place we eventually come to in the Lord, at which we have reached the end of what we can do. By this I do not mean what we can do merely by our carnal ability or by our education. But, even in our ministry, which is given to us by God, we come to a place, by divine appointment, where we can do no more. The trouble with many people is that they have never recognized it.

What follows in this book is the result of God's dealings with me over a number of years, and I am sure that God has not finished His dealings. I will proceed by giving you a number of Scriptures, and then I will use a number of illustrations of "the grace of yielding" and its importance in the Christian life.

One

The Measure of
Spiritual Strength

One

The Measure of Spiritual Strength

The first Scripture I want to examine in regard to our topic is found in Romans 15:1: *"We then that are strong ought to bear the infirmities of the weak, and not to please ourselves."* This, I believe, is the scriptural mark of strength. It's not how much you can do, but rather how much you can bear of the weaknesses of others.

It is very satisfying to be strong in your own ability, in your own ministry, in your own experience—to be the man with all the answers. But that does not really require much spiritual strength. However, it does require spiritual strength to bear the weaknesses of others.

I believe that spiritual strength is measured by God and by the Scriptures in proportion to the amount that we are able to support and bear the weaknesses of other people. For me, personally, that has never been easy.

This is exactly the opposite of the spirit of this age. The spirit of the age is, "Get what you can for yourself. Let the weak take care of themselves."

I have been meditating recently on the whole question of abortion, which to me is a most horrible, hateful evil. But if you discuss this issue with some people, they will justify it on the grounds that many unwanted children are not born into the world—maybe illegitimate children or children that are the result of problem homes or unsuitable mothers—they are just never born. We kill them off before they come out of the womb.

I have learned by experience, regardless of what the Supreme Court or anybody else may say, that

God classifies that as murder. I have learned this by experience, and I also believe it is very clearly unfolded in Scripture.

But the point I want to make just now is this: Once we begin to make what suits us the measure of what is right, we are on a slippery path that goes downward into a horrible mess. Very, very quickly, other issues will follow: "What about the child who is born hopelessly handicapped, who will never be more than a vegetable? Why should we keep that child alive?"

Already, there is a case before the courts in the state of California, involving parents who deliberately did not feed a child who was born hopelessly incapacitated—they just allowed it to die. But, when we have begun to deal with the handicapped in this way, we will then proceed to deal the same way with the aged, the mentally ill, and so on. One after another, they will be written off in the name of humanity.

I want to point out to you that this is *not* the Christian answer. It is not the Christian answer, not merely because abortion is forbidden by God, but also because the attitude behind it is completely unchristian. As Christians, we do not just write off the weak. We don't even relegate them to an institution where we never hear about them or care about them again.

One of the outstanding marks of Christians in the first century was that they cared for the weak. They cared for the sick. They didn't write them off. That is what really impressed the ancient world. The world could not understand what made these Christians concerned about people who had nothing to offer—people who were only liabilities. But I have come to see that if we write off the human liabilities, that is not strength—that is weakness.

The people who are liabilities, the incapacitated, the infirm, and the weak believers, are the test of our spiritual strength. We have obviously come to a place in the United States, and in other countries, too, where we cannot permit ourselves to live by the established standards of the age.

If I'm a Christian, my first motive is not to get away with as much as I can legally get away with.

My first motive is to please Jesus Christ in all that I do. Once we begin to live by seeking to please Jesus, we will inevitably lead a life that is completely different from that of the unconverted around us. We won't need to peddle a lot of doctrine, for, in itself, pleasing Jesus will make us different.

Two

Denying Ourselves

Two

Denying Ourselves

ecall our text from Romans, in which Paul said, *"We...ought...not to please ourselves"* (Romans 15:1). Do you know what I have learned? I have learned that every time I want to do anything effective for God, anything that is acceptable to Him, I begin by not pleasing myself. I have discovered that this is an invariable rule: Every time I am pleasing myself, I am doing nothing that is worth anything to God.

The first thing I have to do is deny myself. This ego in me that is always asserting itself, saying, "I want; I wish; I feel; I think; if you ask me, that's what I like," has to be denied. I have to say, "No!"

There is no problem about what it means to deny yourself, for to deny is to say no. All you have to do is say no to yourself. If you don't say no to yourself and *keep* saying no to yourself, you cannot lead a Christian life. You cannot be a self-pleaser and a Christ-pleaser. It's impossible.

These are the words of Jesus in Luke 9:23:

> *And he said to them all, If **any man** [this is absolutely universal] will come after me, let him deny himself, and take up his cross daily, and follow me.* (emphasis added)

What is the first thing you do when you decide to follow Jesus? What is the first step? Well, Jesus says, *"Let him"*—do what? *"Deny himself."* You cannot begin to follow Jesus until you make that decision.

And then He goes on, *"And take up his cross daily."* I never liked that word *"daily."* For a long while I steered clear of that verse in Luke 9, because I knew another verse that does not have the word *daily* in it. That verse is Matthew 16:24, where the same words are used, but without the *daily*.

At that time in my life, my theology and my teaching were all built on a once-and-for-all experience of the Cross, which is perfectly correct and theological. But my former understanding couldn't exhaust the whole experience of taking up one's cross. And here in Luke 9:23, Jesus sneaks in that little *daily*: *"Let him…take up his cross **daily**."* I believe every day presents every Christian with an opportunity to take up his cross. If you use the opportunity, you have a victorious day. If you lose the opportunity, you have a day of defeat.

But what is your cross? I heard a fellow preacher say it this way: "Your cross is where your will and the will of God cross." Your cross is the thing on which you can die. It's the place where you can lay down your life. When Jesus went to the cross, He said,

> *No man taketh* [my life] *from me, but I lay it down of myself. I have power to lay it down, and I have power to take it again.* (John 10:18)

In this sense, no one will take your life from you. If you don't lay it down voluntarily, you'll still be in control of it.

Your cross, dear brother, is not your wife—unless you have power to lay her down and take her up day by day. Nor, dear lady, is it your husband. Nor is it the sickness you did not choose and cannot be healed of. Your cross is the place where you can make the decision not to please yourself.

I could tell you how, time after time after time in my own experience, when I've had that inner struggle and have made the right decision, blessing has followed. Then, and not until then, I have been able to minister. I cannot minister as long as I am pleasing myself. The old ego in me has nothing to give to anybody. It has to be dealt with before the ministry of God can flow out of my life. And Jesus reminds us, "You need to do it every day." (See Luke 9:23.)

Many, many times in the day, we come to situations where God's will and our wills cross. We have to see those crossings as God-given opportunities—not disasters, but opportunities. I can assure you that, because I am writing this book, I will be given plenty of opportunity to practice it in the days to come. Both God and the Devil will see to that. As a matter of fact, I even thought twice before beginning to write, because I know full well that I'll be tested on what I teach.

Three

The Spirit of Christ

Three

The Spirit of Christ

This principle of taking up your cross and denying yourself daily is exactly the opposite of the way our natural minds work. It is diametrically opposed to the way the natural man thinks. In this chapter, I will give you two other Scriptures that I find very challenging, very searching.

The first Scripture I'll give, without going into its background or analyzing the content, is 1 Corinthians 1:25:

> *The foolishness of God is wiser than men; and the weakness of God is stronger than men.*

Now, that's a paradox! There is a weakness that comes from God that is stronger than any strength we have. There is a foolishness that comes from God that is wiser than any wisdom we have. And there was one thing in which the weakness and the foolishness of God found their full expression. What was that? *The Cross!* In both the weakness and foolishness of the Cross, God triumphed over all the strength and all the wisdom of this world. I believe God is asking you and me to learn that kind of weakness and that kind of foolishness.

It has never been an effort for me to be strong in my own personality. Furthermore, God has blessed and used the strength I have. But God has shown me that my strength and my personality will only take me so far. If I wish, I can stop there. I am not compelled to go any further. But I have seen many lives and ministries stopped at that point.

Now, let's turn to another verse that touches on this, Romans 8:9:

> *But ye are not in the flesh, but in the Spirit, if so be that the Spirit of God dwell in you. Now*

if any man have not the Spirit of Christ, he is none of his.

This verse is strangely constructed. It consists of two distinct sentences. If I had been responsible for the division of the passage into verses, I would have made two separate verses out of these two sentences.

As it stands, the first half of the verse speaks about *"the Spirit of God";* the second half speaks about *"the Spirit of Christ."* I don't wish for a moment to suggest that there is any kind of division between these two, but I do believe there is a difference in the way they represent the nature of God.

All through the Bible, "the Spirit of God" is identified with the Holy Spirit. It is the official title of the third person of the Godhead: God the Spirit, the One who is coequal with the Father and the Son and who speaks in the first person as God. For example, in Acts 13:2, the Holy Spirit spoke to the leaders of the church at Antioch and said, *"Separate **me** Barnabas and Saul for the work whereunto **I** have called them"* (emphasis added). Here we have

God Himself, God the Spirit, using the pronoun *I*, speaking in the first person as God. The main emphasis is upon power and authority.

On the other hand, I believe "the Spirit of Christ" presents the divine nature specifically as it was manifested in the life of Jesus Christ. It cannot be separated from the nature and personality of Jesus. It is this kind of Spirit, Paul told us, that marks the true child of God: *"If any man have not the Spirit of Christ, he is none of his"* (Romans 8:9).

I believe—in fact, I know from direct observation—that there are many people who have been baptized in the Holy Spirit, who speak in tongues, who work miracles, but who demonstrate little or nothing of the Spirit of Christ. And the mark that makes us God's is not speaking in tongues, nor is it working miracles, nor is it preaching tremendous sermons. It is having the Spirit of Christ.

If I were to ask myself what the Spirit of Christ is like, I would have to say it is a meek spirit; it is a humble spirit; it is a gentle spirit. It certainly is not arrogant, self-assertive, or self-pleasing. And that, I believe, is what marks the true child of God: the Spirit of Christ.

We hear a good deal of teaching about claiming your inheritance, and getting what belongs to you. I've preached along that line many times myself, using such texts as 3 John 1:2: *"Beloved, I wish above all things that thou mayest prosper and be in health, even as thy soul prospereth."* Thank God, I believe it!

But do you know that in God's sight you don't prosper by asserting your rights? The Spirit of Jesus did not lay claim to His rights. I believe prosperity, health, inward peace, and well-being of soul are the rights of the new creation, but many times they are illegally appropriated by the old man for his own selfish purposes.

Today, when I hear people say, "Brother, just claim it," something in me winces. When I hear those words, inwardly I picture an arrogant ego asserting its rights. I would like to ask you, How many of you would really like to live with somebody who is always "just claiming it"? Although all my claims may be fully legal, I am inwardly weary of the legalistic assertion of my inheritance in Christ.

I am weary, too, of continually having to instruct Christians on how to be healthy and how to prosper. Certainly, they need it; but, brother and sister, even when you learn how to be healthy and how to prosper, you still are not out of grade school, spiritually. Your strength is not what you have or what you can demonstrate. Rather, your strength is the ability to bear the infirmities of the weak.

Now, the Spirit of Christ is a Spirit that freely yielded. Indeed, I believe that He is the supreme example of yielding. It was just this aspect of His conduct that most clearly marked the difference between Him and Satan. In Philippians 2:6, the Scriptures say about Jesus, *"Who, being in the form of God, thought it not robbery to be equal with God."* That is the King James Version. But the *New American Standard Bible* says, *"He...did not regard equality with God a thing to be grasped."*

Do you see that our lives are in complete and specific contrast to this? Jesus was entitled to equality with God. It was His divine nature, by divine right. He did not grasp at it. Lucifer, who became Satan, was not entitled to equality with God, but he did grasp at it, and he fell. The decisive point of difference was between grasping and yielding. It causes me great consternation when I think how much of our assertion and claiming and demanding is the expression of the Spirit of Christ and how much comes from the other source instead.

I am convinced that the charismatic movement is going to have to face this issue. We are going to have to discern between true and false prophets, true and false ministries, those who are serving God in spirit and truth, and those who are not. Miracles are not the decisive point of difference. The mark that separates is the Spirit of Christ: *"If any man have not the Spirit of Christ, he is none of his"* (Romans 8:9).

Do you know what I believe about the charismatic movement? I believe it's just an interval between two waves. One wave has been going out; another wave is coming in. In between, there is a mess, isn't there? A churning up, a lot of dirt and mire churned up, a kind of confusion, two forces going in opposite directions. That's the charismatic movement! It is not God's ultimate plan. Believe me, something else is coming that is going to be orderly, disciplined, Christ-honoring; and it's going to promote humility, brotherly love, and each believer esteeming others better than himself.

As far as I'm concerned, the day of God's individual man of faith and power is on the way out. I say that without being critical of any man who may ever have qualified for that title. We need to realize that God works in different ways at different times. He doesn't go on forever doing the same thing. Some Christians are not prepared to accept that. They find a success formula that works, and they go on until they've worked it to death.

I am reminded of what Paul said to the men of Athens in Acts 17:30. Speaking about their many, many centuries of idolatry, he said, *"The times of this ignorance God winked at."* To wink is to close your eyes for a brief moment. So, for a brief moment, God voluntarily overlooked that ignorance.

Many people argue, "Well, God let me get away with it for ten years, so I'm going to go on getting away with it." No, you aren't! God winked at it, but now He has opened both His eyes; He's looking right at it, and He's saying, "You'd better change." And when God says, "You'd better change," my advice is: Change! If you don't, God has ways of making sure you understand the lesson.

Four

Being Willing to Yield

Four

Being Willing to Yield

*N*ow I want to look at some examples of yielding, beginning with 1 Kings 3. In the first part of this chapter, God appears to Solomon in a dream and says, *"Ask what I shall give thee"* (verse 5). That would be a pretty difficult situation to find yourself in, when God suddenly says, "Now what do you want? I'll give it to you."

You will remember that Solomon did not ask for riches; he did not ask for honor; he did not ask for the lives of his enemies; he asked for wisdom. He said, *"Give* [me] *an understanding heart to judge thy people, that I may discern between good and bad"* (1 Kings 3:9). God was pleased with this choice and said,

> *Because thou hast asked this thing,…I have also given thee that which thou hast not asked, both riches, and honour.* (verses 11, 13)

Shortly after this event, there came the case of the two women who were harlots, living together in one house. Each of them had given birth to a baby, and each had her baby in bed with her. In the middle of the night one of the women rolled over on top of her own baby and killed it. In the morning there were two mothers and only one baby, and each of the mothers wanted the baby that was alive. Both the real mother and the mother whose baby had died claimed the baby.

So the case was brought before Solomon: these two women in court, and one baby. Solomon heard the case out. The real mother said, "It's my baby." The other woman said, "No, it's my baby." So

Solomon said, "Well, there's only one thing to do. Bring me a sword." When the sword came, he said, "I'll cut the baby in two, and each of you can have half." The woman to whom the baby did not belong said, "That's right, cut the baby in half and give me my half." But the real mother did not want to see her baby die, and she said, "No, give her the baby; let it live." And by this, Solomon identified the real mother. As a result, his wisdom became famous throughout Israel.

The lesson is very simple. If the baby is really yours, rather than see it die, you will let the other woman have it. That is the real test. Many times in Christian service and ministry, a man brings forth something that is his, but somebody else contests it and claims it, and there's an argument and a fight. I could go through the history of the last thirty years and name man after man and case after case. That's when the real test comes. If it's your child, would you rather see the other woman have it than see it be killed?

There are times when we are put to that test. Do I want to lay claim to my ministry and my success;

do I want to establish my reputation? Or am I prepared to let somebody else have all that I worked
for, all that I achieved, all that I prayed through? It
depends on whether you love yourself more than the
baby, or the baby more than yourself.

Next time you're faced with that situation, you
will be able to measure how real your love is. If
you're willing to give it away, you love it. If you claim
half of it, you don't love it.

Look for a moment at the story of Abraham
in the thirteenth chapter of Genesis. Abraham had
started out from Ur of the Chaldees in obedience to
the word of God, but not in full obedience. We see
this from the twelfth chapter of Genesis. There God
said,

> *Get thee out of thy country, and from thy kin-*
> *dred, and from thy father's house, unto a land*
> *that I will show thee.* (verse 1)

But Abraham did not fully obey God, because
he took two extra persons with him—his father and
his nephew. He was not authorized to take either. As

long as he had his father with him, he got only half-way. He got to Haran, which is halfway between Ur and Canaan. He couldn't get any farther until his father died.

Many of us are like that. God says, "Come out; leave everything behind; I'll show you your inheritance." But we want to take "Daddy" along. Daddy may be a promising career or a well-paid job or a denominational affiliation or a pension scheme. It may be one of many things. At any rate, God says, "As long as you take Daddy, you'll get only halfway." That's how it was with Abraham. He couldn't get into Canaan as long as he had his father with him. Stephen pointed this out in his speech to the Jewish council in Acts 7. He said, "After his father died, he moved into the promised land." (See verse 4.)

But, even so, Abraham still had a problem—his nephew, Lot. Lot never should have been there.

It wasn't long before both Abraham and Lot prospered. They both acquired so much cattle and so many goods that they could no longer live side by side as they had been doing. There was continual strife between their herdsmen. We read what happened next in Genesis 13, beginning at verse 7:

> *And there was a strife between the herdmen of Abram's [Abraham's] cattle and the herdmen of Lot's cattle: and the Canaanite and the Perizzite dwelled then in the land. And Abram said unto Lot, Let there be no strife, I pray thee, between me and thee, and between my herdmen and thy herdmen; for we be brethren. Is not the whole land before thee? separate thyself, I pray thee, from me: if thou wilt take the left hand, then I will go to the right; or if thou depart to the right hand, then I will go to the left.* (Genesis 13:7–9)

Abraham was the senior; he was the man whom God had called; he was the man to whom the inheritance belonged. But he stood back and said, "Lot, you make your choice. Whatever you choose, you can have."

> *And Lot lifted up his eyes, and beheld all the plain of Jordan, that it was well watered every where, before the LORD destroyed Sodom and Gomorrah, even as the garden of the LORD,*

like the land of Egypt, as thou comest unto Zoar. Then Lot chose him all the plain of Jordan; and Lot journeyed east: and they separated themselves the one from the other. Abram dwelled in the land of Canaan, and Lot dwelled in the cities of the plain, and pitched his tent toward Sodom. But the men of Sodom were wicked and sinners before the LORD exceedingly. (Genesis 13:10–13)

Now, continue reading about what happened after Lot was separated from Abraham:

And the LORD said unto Abram, after that Lot was separated from him, Lift up now thine eyes, and look from the place where thou art northward, and southward, and eastward, and westward: for all the land which thou seest, to thee will I give it, and to thy seed for ever. (verses 14–15)

That was his inheritance, but God didn't show it to him until he had been willing to yield.

That's how God will deal with us, too. As long as you hold on and say, "That's mine; I'm not letting go," you won't see what God has for you. It's

the yielding spirit that receives the inheritance—not
the grasping spirit or the grabbing spirit. As long as
you continue to say, "It's mine, and you can't have
it; God gave it to me," you won't have what God has
for you. You have to yield.

My wife Lydia often reminded me of an inci-
dent that happened in Palestine during World War II,
before we were married. She was living at that time
in a children's home in a town named Ramallah,
which is about ten miles north of Jerusalem. Though
most of her ministry was with children, a revival
broke out among the Arab women in the city. It was
a sovereign work of God, but my wife was the instru-
ment that God used. Those Arab women would come
in off the street unconverted, to be saved, delivered
from evil spirits, and baptized in the Holy Spirit—all
in the one encounter. The work was flourishing and
growing, a testimony to the Lord's grace.

But then, a missionary who lived in Jerusalem
claimed the work as his. He sent up an Arab worker
and said, "This is our work. We had a worker in
this town before you came." In actual fact, that
particular worker had accomplished nothing of

any lasting value, whereas my wife understood and loved those women and was loved by them. I bear testimony to this because, twenty-five years later, we went back to that village, my wife and I together, and when these women heard that my wife was there, they came running into the street to embrace her. They had not forgotten her, twenty-five years later!

Be that as it may, my wife was confronted with this claim, and with the strength of a man against a single woman. So she said what Abraham said: "All right, you choose. And if you decide to go to the left, I'll go to the right." And the other missionary said, "Well, this is our work; we'll take it."

So my wife said to the Arab women, "From now on, we're having no meetings. The meetings are to be held at such and such a place; you go there and be faithful and support the work." After a year or two, the work died completely, because the worker who was sent to take it over had no real call from God. It was not his work. But my wife had won her own personal victory by yielding.

Meanwhile, within a few months, British and American soldiers serving in the countries of the Middle East began to find their way to that little home in Ramallah. They came there seeking God and the baptism of the Holy Spirit. In the next three or four years, scores and scores of American and British servicemen found God and were baptized in the Holy Spirit in that little home for children.

As a matter of fact, I myself was with the British forces in the Middle East at that time. I was stationed in the Sudan, which is almost right in the center of Africa. One day I met another Christian soldier who said, "If you want a real blessing, there's a little children's home ten miles north of Jerusalem—you should go there!" So, as soon as my turn came, I took two weeks' leave and journeyed all the way up, or rather down, the Nile to Cairo, and from there to Jerusalem. Finally, I ended up in that little children's home, and the blessing I got was greater than I had been expecting—it was my wife!

But the point of the story is this: By traditions and customs of the Middle East, those Arab women would never have been allowed in a place where British and American servicemen were coming. Had my wife held on to the women, the soldiers would never have come. But, when we yield, then we get promoted. Many of those men, myself included, today are in full-time ministry all over the world. They are missionaries, pastors, and so on—some in the United States, some in Britain, some in South Africa.

The lesson is this: You have to be willing to let go. You may say, "It's unfair; it's unreasonable; it's unjust!" So what? God arranged it. He's in control. That's faith!

Five

"Take Now Thy Son..."

Five

"Take Now Thy Son..."

Now, let's go back to Abraham. One thing that has become very clear to me is that faith is not a static condition. It's not sitting on a church pew and saying, "I've got it." Faith is a walk in which one step follows another.

Abraham is called the father of all who believe, but we are only his children if we walk in the steps of his faith. We can find, in Romans 4, the steps that he took. Abraham's faith was progressive. If you go from Genesis 12 to Genesis 22, you will see the various progressions of Abraham's faith. In chapter twenty-two, his faith came to its grand climax. But what he did in chapter twenty-two, he never could have done in chapter twelve. His faith came to that climax because every time God said, "Step," he stepped. Every time God gave him a challenge, he accepted. So his faith was progressively built up.

The epistle of James says, "By works his faith was developed and made mature." (See James 2:22.) Faith is received as a gift, but it is matured by walking in steps of obedience.

However, Abraham was human like the rest of us. He, too, made his mistakes. God had promised him a child of his own—an heir to take over his inheritance. But, as you know, the promise tarried. After twelve years, no heir had appeared. Sarah was seventy-eight years old, and she viewed the situation as hopeless. Finally she said, "If we're ever going to have a child, we'd better do something about it." (See Genesis 16:1–2.) When we deal with God, some of the most disastrous words that we can ever utter are, "We'd better do something about it."

Anyhow, Abraham took his wife's advice (which was a mistake) and had a child by Sarah's maid, Hagar. There was nothing immoral about that whatsoever. By the standards of the day, it was right, moral, and decent. But it wasn't the plan of God. The name of the child was Ishmael, and his descendants are numbered among the Arabs of the Middle East today.

Later, Sarah herself gave birth to Isaac, the child whom God had really intended her to have all along. And for the past four thousand years, there has been tension between the descendants of these two children—Ishmael and Isaac—tension that seems to be coming to its climax in our day. By the irony of history, the descendants of Ishmael, or the Arabs, now stand as the great barrier to the descendants of Isaac, or the Israelites, returning to their promised inheritance. History could not teach a plainer lesson: It is disastrous to grasp for a God-given inheritance by carnal means.

I heard another preacher say this: "The child of human expediency is an Ishmael." When you decide you'd better do something to help God, God help you!

I was planning something last year, and I went quite a long way in my plans. Then I got together with a fellow minister, and as we were talking it over, I said, "To tell you the truth, I don't think I'm going to do it."

He said, "Why not?"

"Well," I said, "I'm afraid it will be an Ishmael." I saw that my friend was impressed by that remark.

Some time later we were together again and he said, "Would you mind telling me why you changed your mind about doing that thing?"

"It was the fear of the Lord," I told him. And I saw that the answer satisfied him. I can sincerely say that I try to live in the fear of the Lord. I do not want to do anything that grieves God, that stands in God's way. I want to walk softly with the Lord. So, I put my Ishmael in the pending file—which is where it is today!

To me, the basic lesson is this: The things that we think are good, the things that seem right and that are the result of human attempts to do the right thing, are the biggest disasters. God keep us from them! God keep me from them! God keep you from them! God keep all of us from ever begetting an Ishmael because, brothers and sisters, we will live to regret it.

What is the biggest test that God ever puts us through? I can tell you in one word that begins with a *w:* Waiting! That's right! When God tells you to climb the mountain, you start climbing immediately! But when God tells you to sit at the bottom and wait, you can't do it.

Probably the most mature character in the Bible is Moses. How did he mature? By forty years in the wilderness. What did it make him? The meekest man on earth. Moses didn't assert his rights; he stepped back and said, "Let somebody else do it." I feel safe when I can say with all sincerity, "Let somebody else have the baby." Oh, I feel so safe! But when I'm nervous, tense, and grasping, I'm headed for disaster.

Now, let us go back to Genesis 22. God said to Abraham in verse 2,

> *Take now thy son, thine only son Isaac, whom thou lovest, and get thee into the land of Moriah; and offer him there for a burnt offering upon one of the mountains which I will tell thee of.*

What was Abraham's response? The next verse tells us: *"And Abraham rose up early in the morning, and saddled his ass"* (verse 3).

One of the things you'll notice about Abraham is that he did not merely obey God, but he obeyed God promptly. This is very conspicuous. When he was told to do something, he got up early the next morning and did it. He didn't wait around until noon, wondering if God would change His mind. When God gave this command to Abraham, the next morning Abraham was up and on his way with Isaac for the three-day journey to Mount Moriah.

You know the story. They went up the mountain, and Isaac said, "My father, here's the fire, and here's the wood, but where's the lamb?" (See Genesis 22:7.) And Abraham said, *"My son, God will provide...a lamb"* (verse 8). In the eleventh chapter of Hebrews, the writer tells us that it was by faith that Abraham was willing to offer his son to God and kill him, *"accounting that God was able to raise him up, even from the dead"* (verse 19).

If you read the twenty-second chapter of Genesis carefully, you will understand why the writer of Hebrews said that. It is because Abraham said to the men whom he left at the foot of the mountain, "My son and I will go up, *we* will worship, and *we* will come down." (See Genesis 22:5.) Bless God! Abraham really believed that even if he thrust that knife into his son, both of them would come down again. He had come to the place where he was actually ready to kill the miracle child who was the only hope of his God-promised inheritance, trusting God to bring him back to life again.

When he had the knife raised, ready to plunge it into his son, the angel of God called to him from heaven and stopped him (Genesis 22:11). Abraham discovered that God had, indeed, provided an alternative sacrifice: a ram caught by its horns in a thicket. He offered that up to God in place of his son. After that, God spoke to him the second time:

> *And the angel of the* Lord *called unto Abraham out of heaven the second time, and said, By myself have I sworn, saith the* Lord [the writer of Hebrews says He swore by Himself because He could not swear by anything greater (see Hebrews 6:13)], *for because thou hast done this thing, and hast not withheld thy son, thine only son: that in blessing I will bless thee, and in multiplying I will multiply thy seed as the stars of the heaven.*
> (verses 15–17)

That's a strange thing, isn't it? Isaac was God's gift to Abraham and Sarah. They never could have had him apart from the miraculous intervention of God.

He was supernaturally born. Yet the very child that God had given them, God asked them to give back to Him as a burnt sacrifice.

I have often been quite occupied with the picture of Abraham on his way to Mount Moriah. I've tried to put myself in his position and imagine what he was reasoning and thinking on the three-day journey. And I can imagine the questions that came to Abraham's mind: Why would God want Isaac? Didn't God give Isaac to us? Isn't he the promised one? Isn't he the only way that we'll ever receive our God-given inheritance? Haven't we left everything? Haven't we followed Him? Haven't we obeyed Him? Why should He demand Isaac?

I don't know whether he thought that or said that. But when he came to the place where he was willing to do what God had commanded, God spoke and said, "That's all right; now I know your heart. From now on, Abraham, I'll bless you as you've never been blessed before, and I will multiply your seed." What was his seed? Isaac. See the lesson? If he had held on to Isaac, all he'd have had was Isaac.

When he gave Isaac up, He got Isaac back, multiplied beyond his power to calculate.

I've seen that this is what happens when God gives us something very special for ourselves. It's from God. It's precious. It's unique. It's miraculous. But one day God is going to say, "I want it. Give it back. Kill it. Lay it on the altar." At that point, you're either going to follow in the footsteps of Abraham, or you're going to miss God's blessing.

I have to say that I've seen many servants of the Lord make the bitter mistake of holding on to their Isaac, and all they are left with is Isaac. That is the biggest test that comes to any servant of God: Is he willing to put his ministry on the altar?

I can look back and see how I faced this test in my own experience. Many of you know how I became deeply involved in the ministry of deliverance and was publicly identified with it across this nation. I can echo the words of Paul and say that I've fought with wild beasts (see 1 Corinthians 15:32) for the truth of deliverance. I have fought physically; I have fought spiritually; I have fought in prayer; I have fought in fasting.

But there came a time when God joined me with three other men who had nationally known teaching ministries. God sovereignly brought us together in a relationship of mutual commitment and submission. This was a sovereign dealing of God with each and all of us—not anything that we had planned or expected, or that we even really understood. In that sense, I would have to say, it bore the marks of an Isaac, not an Ishmael.

It wasn't long before I realized that my ministry of deliverance was included in the commitment I had made to my brothers. It had to be submitted to them. After much heart searching, I finally said to them, "Brothers, if you find that my ministry of deliverance is unscriptural or wrong and you take exception to it, I will not practice it." Do you think that didn't cost something? It did!

But today I praise God for the results that flowed from it. First of all, my brothers never asked me to give up practicing deliverance. On the contrary, they supported me and strengthened me. When I was publicly attacked, they stood by me, often at the cost of their own reputations.

But beyond all that, something happened to the ministry of deliverance across this nation that I never could have achieved by my own efforts. When I gave God my Isaac, He multiplied it. Today, the ministry of deliverance has been established in almost every area of this nation. I can go almost anywhere in the United States and preach deliverance, and there are qualified, dedicated men of God who will do the work. In fact, I very seldom have to minister deliverance myself any longer.

God has raised up an army of men who are willing and able to practice it. But believe me, it wasn't that way a few decades ago! Looking back now, I thank God that I was willing to give Him my Isaac and let Him multiply it. I believe that if I had held on to my Isaac, I would be left today with just my own ministry, isolated from the body of Christ and from the mainstream of God's purposes.

Let's look in John 12:24 at the words of Jesus:

Verily, verily, I say unto you, Except a corn of wheat fall into the ground and die, it abideth alone: but if it die, it bringeth forth much fruit.

I have always applied that verse to the death of Christ, and there is no doubt that it does apply. Jesus was the corn of wheat; He was willing to lay down His life. He fell into the ground and was buried, and out of His death and burial and resurrection, there came forth much fruit.

But just recently, as I have been meditating on the things I have written in this book, I have begun to see myself and my fellow believers, each one of us, holding in our hands a little corn of wheat that God has placed there: our gifts, our ministries, our talents, things that are precious because God has given them to us.

You may say, "It's mine; I can do it. I know how to cast out demons. I can pray for the sick, and they get smitten to the ground. I have the word of knowledge." It is so nice to hold your gift in your hand and feel it there and say, "It's mine." But God says, "If you keep it there, that's all you'll have—just one little corn." You can put your name on it; you can put your label on it; you can go on claiming it as yours, but you'll never get more.

But, what is the alternative? Let go! Drop it! "You mean, let my ministry go? Let my talent go? Let my gift go?" Yes, let it go! Let it go right down into the earth and get buried and lost. Let it go out of sight. After that, you won't own it any longer. Instead, God will be responsible for it. And God has guaranteed the fruit.

I believe this is the place to which we're coming. Many of us are going to be faced with this choice: Do I want to propagate *myself?* Do I want to establish *my* reputation? Do I want to build *my* ministry, *my* outreach, *my* camp, *my* youth center, *my* deliverance center? Am I interested in the fact that it's *mine?* Or, if I'm wrongfully challenged and the ownership is disputed, am I willing to say to the wrongful mother, "You take it"? Do I love it, or do I love me?

These are very searching questions. Whatever God has given you, I believe there will come a time when He will ask you to let it go. Drop it. Let it fall.

"Take Now Thy Son..."

You will be glad that you let it go! I'm glad I've let
some things go, too. If I had gone on carrying them,
they would have dragged me down to the ground.

Six

"Except a Corn of Wheat..."

Six

"Except a Corn of Wheat..."

*M*ost preachers are too busy. I'm busy, but I'm not too busy. Did you know that it isn't spiritual to be too busy? It may impress people, but it's not spiritual. God made you only one person, and you'll never do two people's jobs satisfactorily, no matter how hard you try.

I read a little article by Jamie Buckingham in his church bulletin about his decision to give up doing the "urgent" in order to do the "important." Most preachers are so submerged beneath the urgent, they never get to do what is important. One of the most needed prayers to be found in the Bible is in Psalm 90: *"Teach us to number our days, that we may apply our hearts unto wisdom"* (verse 12). In other words, "Teach me how to use my time."

That is one of the things that impresses me most about Jesus. He was never flustered. He was never hurried. He was never too busy. Actually, it's an extension of my ego if I make myself indispensable. Most people really don't want to be dispensable. As far as I'm concerned, my greatest triumph is when I can be done without. Then I've succeeded!

There is a true story that relates to this. It's so personal that I'll have to be careful. But the out-working of it is going on in my life all the time. In June 1971, I went to Seattle, Washington, to take part in a kind of fellowship retreat for ministers. Don Basham was there, as well as Bob Mumford, Charles Simpson, Larry Christenson, Ralph Wilkerson, David DuPlessis, Dennis Bennett, Ern Baxter, and many other nationally known charismatic teachers.

The retreat lasted about five days. Every morning and most of the afternoons we were gathered in fellowship, and it was quite an experience. We spent a day and a half talking about demons. We spent two days talking about water baptism. When you've cleared those two hurdles, you've made progress!

Nevertheless, to get so many teachers to the far northwestern corner of the United States was very expensive, and they had no funds from which to draw. So the organizers of the conference said, "Brothers in Christ, we promise you nothing, but we'll try to raise the money for your fares." For this purpose they arranged public services every night of the week in five strategic points in and around Seattle. And they turned loose two or three preachers every night at each point. Well, every one of those places was filled to capacity every night before the meeting ever opened. And the response of the people was tremendous.

When the retreat was over, I stayed on in Seattle to minister in one of the Assemblies of God churches, just for the weekend. In this way, I had the opportunity to hear the local ministers talking together about the meetings. As I had previously pastored a church in Seattle, I knew many of them, and I knew that they were expressing their real opinions. In essence, their comments amounted to this: "In all our memories, no meetings have ever made such an impact on the city of Seattle as these meetings." But the comical thing about those meetings, from the human standpoint, was that they weren't organized to make an impact on the city of Seattle. They were organized to raise money for the preachers' fares. That's the simple truth!

On Monday morning I found myself on a plane, flying from Seattle to Atlanta, where my next meetings were scheduled. A plane is one of the best places to meditate. The telephone can't reach you; people don't bother you; you just sit back in your seat, alone with your thoughts. As I sat there, I began to say to myself, "Isn't that strange? Meetings that were not planned to make an impact on a city made a greater impact than meetings that were planned for that very purpose."

At that moment, the Lord began to speak to me very clearly—not audibly, but quietly and very definitely—and this is what He said: "Now tell Me this. With whom did I have more problems—Jonah or the city of Nineveh?" I thought for a while, and then I said, "Lord, when You got Jonah straightened out, You had no problems with Nineveh." And He said, "And when I get the preachers straightened out, I'll have no problems with the people!"

Now, I can tell that story because I'm a preacher myself. The Lord didn't say, "When I get the other preachers straightened out"; He said, "When I get the preachers straightened out." I was included with the rest of them, and I realized that.

After I had reached Atlanta, the Lord continued to deal with me along this line. My meetings there were being held in a hotel. Between two of the meetings, I was resting on a bed in one of the rooms, and my mind was more or less blank. I find that when our minds are not too active, God can more easily get our attention. As I lay there in that condition, a series of words came to my mind, many of them place names. They were as clear and as vivid as if they had been printed on paper before my eyes.

These were the words: "From Cherith to Zarephath; from Zarephath to Carmel; from Carmel to Horeb; and from Horeb into many lives." I knew enough of the Bible to recognize immediately that the words were an outline of the career of Elijah and that the place names represented successive stages in his ministry: from Cherith to Zarephath to Carmel to Horeb.

Then I began to fill in the details in my mind and saw very plainly that the real climax of Elijah's public ministry was on Mount Carmel. (See 1 Kings 18:19–40.) It was there that he gathered all Israel; there he challenged 850 false prophets; there he called down fire from heaven and saw all Israel prostrated on their faces, crying, *"The Lord, he is the God"* (verse 39). If ever any man had a personal, individual triumph, that man was Elijah on Mount Carmel.

But then the Lord showed me that within a few days, Elijah was running away from Jezebel, a woman and a witch, and asking God to take away his life. (See 1 Kings 19:1–4.) So brief and impermanent was the triumph of Carmel! The next thought that came to me was this: Had God answered Elijah's request and taken away his life at that point, Elijah would have died with his task incomplete and without any spiritual successor. There would have been no one to carry on and complete his work. But when he finally got to Horeb and came face-to-face with God and heard God's plan, it was very different from Elijah's plan.

God said, "Elijah, what are you doing here?" (See 1 Kings 19:9, 13.) Then Elijah said, *"I have been very jealous for the LORD"* (verses 10, 14), and he went on to give a list of all his activities and achievements. The Lord said, in so many words, "I know about that, Elijah, but what are you doing here?" And when Elijah had finished telling the Lord all that he had been doing, the Lord told him what He wanted him to do next. He said, "I want you to anoint three men: Elisha to be prophet in your place, Hazael to be king of Syria, and Jehu to be king of Israel." (See verses 15–16.)

If you read the subsequent chapters in 1 and 2 Kings, you will find that those three men, who were the product of that interview between God and Elijah on Mount Horeb, finished off every task assigned by God to Elijah. Eventually, there was nothing left undone. Elijah could not finish the job himself, but he could find his successors and hand it over to them.

As all this passed through my mind, I realized that God was speaking very directly to me. He was showing me that I had two options before me. On the one hand, I could go on doing my own thing, carrying on my own ministry, using the faith and the power that God had given me to whatever extent I was able, and I could achieve some kind of a personal triumph. But I would end without a successor, and there would be no permanent fruit to my ministry.

On the other hand, God showed me the alternative: Don't be ambitious for yourself; don't promote your own ministry; don't do your own thing; rather, invest in the lives of others. Let them get the credit;

let them take over where you have to leave off. Let them be more successful than you are.

I've always been, in a certain sense, a successful person. I don't say that boastfully, but, from way back when I was twelve years old, I've been head boy, captain of the school, senior scholar, youngest fellow of the college—all the way through. It is ingrained in my thinking to expect to be successful. But God has shown me that there is a higher standard of success. Let that little corn of wheat that you hold in your hand fall to the ground and die, and God will take care of the rest.

And so I can tell you that I am possibly the freest person around, because I have "let go and let God." I don't care if I never cast out another demon. If God doesn't want me to, I don't mind that in the least. I don't mind if I never conduct another seminar, if I never write another book. If God so leads that I disappear from the public eye, that's all right by me, as long as I've invested what I have where it will do good.

I don't even know how much I have; I don't have to know. But what I have, I'm willing to give; I'm willing to let it drop out of my hand. As a result, I'm very, very happy. Truly, I am free. I know what it is to *act* free; I know what it is to *preach* freedom; but the best thing is to *be* free. And even as I write this I can say, in all sincerity before God, "I'm free!"

Seven

Letting Go

Seven

Letting Go

et me write just a few more pages before
I finish. I have been gripped recently by
the word *secret,* as it is used in various
places in the Bible. For instance, in 1 Corinthians
2:7, Paul said, *"But we speak the wisdom of God
in a mystery"* (emphasis added). The Revised
Standard Version renders this verse as, *"But we
impart a secret and hidden wisdom of God"*
(emphasis added). So, there is a secret wisdom of
God, something that is hidden from the minds of
most people. For my part, I have a deep desire to
acquire that secret, hidden wisdom!

In Psalm 51:6, David said, *"Behold, thou desirest truth in the inward parts: and in the hidden part thou shalt make me to know wisdom."* Notice the concept of "wisdom in the hidden part," which could be interpreted as "wisdom in the hidden *place.*" In 1 Corinthians 2:7, Paul was probably referring to this wisdom of God that is hidden in a secret place.

To me, there is something specially attractive about all this—the secret place, the secret wisdom, the secret knowledge. But there is one condition we have to meet in order to discover the secret. If a thing is secret, it is hidden; it is out of sight. And so, if we want to dwell in that secret place and find that secret wisdom, we ourselves must be willing to be hidden. Otherwise, our own personalities, our own reputations, our own egos will stand in the way. We will have to let them go—to let them fall into the ground and die.

Think about the life of Jesus for just a moment. Since His incarnation as a man, He has spent about thirty years in perfect family life, three and a half years in public ministry, and about two thousand years in intercession! Are you prepared for that proportion? Do you want to have real influence? The people who rule the world for God are the intercessors, and most of them are not publicly known at all. Are you willing to bow out?

What was the last public appearance of Jesus in the eyes of the world? He was on the cross. Then, when He reappeared in the earth, how did He reappear? In the ministry of His disciples. He fell into the ground and died, and out came the fruit. Are you willing to do that? Am I willing to do that? Are you holding on to your Isaac? "God, You gave it to me," you say. "It's mine." But God says, "Give it back. Put it on the altar. Take the knife." He says, "If you'll give it to Me, in My way, and in My time, when it suits Me, I'll bless it and multiply it more than is in your ability to understand or comprehend."

Years ago, I told the Lord that I would no longer preach merely religious lectures if I could help it; that when I preached, I would give the people an opportunity to act on the truth I had preached. I feel that I owe it to people to do that, and so I owe it to my readers as well. I suppose that many of you are holding on to your Isaacs, saying, "It's mine, God. I built it up; I established it."

Maybe your Isaac is really a literal child that you're holding on to. God says, "Will you let go and let Me?" Or it may be some gift, some ministry, or some special situation. If God has really spoken to your heart through this book, then you now have the opportunity to bring your Isaac and put it on the altar.

You may be unhappy, edgy, or tense because you are asserting your own will and your own claim to something that God has given you. It may be a ministry; it may be a gift; it may be a situation; it may be a person. But God, by His Holy Spirit, will give you the grace to let go and bring that Isaac to Him. Just hand it over to Him, and trust Him with the consequences.

If God has spoken to your heart, bow in prayer. Kneel before God at the altar, and give Him your Isaac. Then you will be able to say with me, "I'm free! I'm truly free!"

About the Author

About the Author

*D*erek Prince (1915–2003) was born in Bangalore, India, into a British military family. He was educated as a scholar of classical languages at Eton College and Cambridge University in England and later at Hebrew University, Israel. As a student, he was a philosopher and self-proclaimed atheist.

While in the British Medical Corps during World War II, Prince began to study the Bible as a philosophical work. Converted through a powerful encounter with Jesus Christ, he was baptized in the Holy Spirit a few days later. This life-changing experience altered the whole course of his life, which he thereafter devoted to studying and teaching the Bible as the Word of God.

Internationally recognized as a Bible scholar and spiritual patriarch, Prince taught and ministered on six continents for over seven decades. Until a few years before his death at the age of 88, he traveled the world, imparting God's revealed truth, praying for the sick and afflicted, and sharing his prophetic insights into world events in the light of Scripture. He wrote over 45 books, which have been translated into over 60 languages and distributed worldwide. He pioneered teaching on such groundbreaking themes as generational curses, the biblical significance of Israel, and demonology.

Derek Prince Ministries, with its international headquarters in Charlotte, North Carolina, continues to distribute his teachings and to train missionaries, church leaders, and congregations through its worldwide branch offices. It is estimated that Derek Prince's clear teaching of the Bible has reached more than half the globe through his books, tapes, and daily radio program, *Keys to Successful Living*. In 2002 he said, "It is my desire—and I believe the Lord's desire—that this ministry continue the work, which God began through me over sixty years ago, until Jesus returns."

The Holy Spirit in You
Derek Prince

Derek Prince clearly explains the ways of the Holy Spirit and how He works in the lives of Christians. Discover how you can, through the power of the Holy Spirit, experience the continual presence of Jesus, become bold a witness for Christ, pray according to God's will, and receive physical and emotional healing. As you understand and receive the active presence of the Spirit in your life, you will gain new power and grace for living.

ISBN: 0-88368-961-8 • Trade • 112 pages

UJ
WHITAKER
HOUSE

proclaiming the power of the Gospel through the written word
visit our website at www.whitakerhouse.com

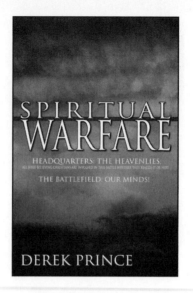

Spiritual Warfare
Derek Prince

Resist the enemy's attacks. Tear down the enemy's
strongholds. Learn the key to victory. Derek Prince
explains the battle that's happening now between
the forces of God and the forces of evil. Choose to
be prepared by learning the enemy's strategies so
you can effectively block his attacks.
We have God on our side,
and nothing will keep us from victory!

ISBN: 0-88368-670-8 • Trade • 144 pages

ய

WHITAKER
HOUSE

proclaiming the power of the Gospel through the written word
visit our website at www.whitakerhouse.com

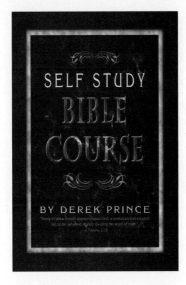

Self-Study Bible Course
Derek Prince

Even if you have never read the Bible before, you will find this study guide helpful and easy to use. Or, if you have been a believer for many years, you will find a new ease in communicating with God, receiving His guidance, and witnessing to others. Through this course, you will experience important changes in your life and discover an intimacy with God that you may have never known before.

ISBN: 0-88368-421-7 • Workbook • 64 pages

WHITAKER HOUSE

proclaiming the power of the Gospel through the written word
visit our website at www.whitakerhouse.com

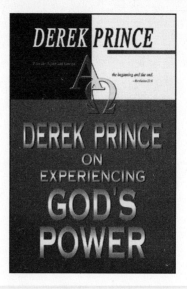

Derek Prince on Experiencing God's Power
Derek Prince

In this anointed collection of several of his best-selling books, author Derek Prince shows how to receive God's promises regarding healing, fasting, marriage, spiritual warfare, finances, prayer, the Holy Spirit, and much more. In this unique and valuable guide, you will find answers to some of life's toughest issues, and you will discover how to achieve powerful results in your spiritual quest.

ISBN: 0-88368-551-5 • Trade • 528 pages

WHITAKER
HOUSE

proclaiming the power of the Gospel through the written word
visit our website at www.whitakerhouse.com